KOJIKI
The Birth of Japan

by Kazumi Wilds

TUTTLE Publishing

Tokyo | Rutland, Vermont | Singapore

All was chaos before the heaven
and the earth came into existence.

All was shapeless mass. Something light and
transparent rose up and formed the heaven.

The world resembled oil floating,
jellyfish-like, upon the face of water.

Then the heavenly deities were born. They were likewise
born alone, and hid themselves. It took millions and millions
of years before the earth was formed.

Like the sprouting of a reed, many more deities were born.
Then Izanagi, the Male-Who-Invites Deity,
and Izanami, the Female-Who-Invites Deity, were born.
All the other heavenly deities summoned Izanagi
and Izanami to consolidate the world,
handing them a spear.

Standing upon the Floating Bridge of Heaven,
Izanagi and Izanami pushed down the spear
and stirred the brine till it went curdle-curdle.
The brine that dripped down from the spear piled up
and became an island.

Wishing to be married,
the two deities
descended to the island
and found a pillar.

Izanagi questioned
Izanami, "How is
your body formed?"

Izanami replied,
"My body is empty
in one place."

Izanagi proclaimed, "My body sticks out in one place. I would like to thrust the part of my body that sticks out into the part of your body that is empty, and fill it up to birth lands."

The children born from Izanagi and Izanami were the land of the Eight Great Islands that became the origin of Japan.

Then they begot deities to preside over the country. Their firstborn proved to be the sea god, next the gods of harbor, then the wind deity, the deity of trees, the deity of mountains, the goddess of the plains, the deity of great food, the deity of communication, and on and on.

Through giving birth to
the deity of fire
her private parts were burnt
and Izanami fell gravely ill.

From her vomit
came the deity of metals,
from her excrement
came the deity of clay,
from her urine
came the deity of
fresh growth.

Izanami eventually died.

Izanagi's hot tears fell like
hailstones and out of the
teardrops was born the
deity of weeping.

In a fit of uncontrollable grief, Izanagi resolved
to go down to the land of Yomi the Underworld
in order to seek his wife and bring her back.

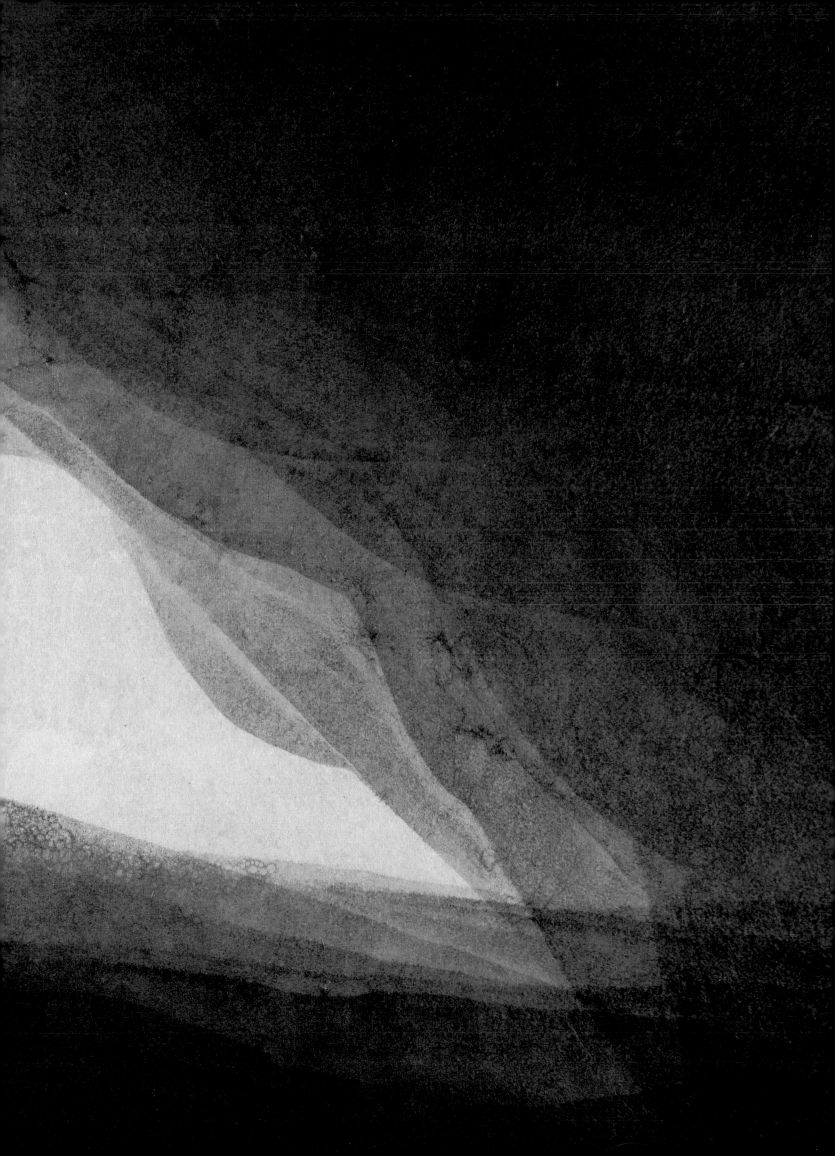

Many millions of miles separated the earth from the
Lower Regions. Izanagi had a long and arduous journey.

There he approached a large castle and he found Izanami
at the gate of an inner court. Izanagi called her to come back
to the world to complete their work of creation.

Izanami replied, "Alas! You have come too late.
I have already eaten food from the furnace of Yomi.
Having once eaten the things of this land,
it is impossible for me to come back to the world."

She lowered her head in
deep despair, and continued,
"I wish to go back with you.
I'll speak to the deities of
Yomi to obtain their permission.
Wait here until my return,
but remember that you must
not on any account look
inside the castle."

Izanagi waited and
waited, but no shadow
of his wife appeared.

The day gradually
wore on and waned away,
darkness was about to fall.

Forgetting the vow he had made
to the goddess, Izanagi stuck his head
into the inner court to see inside,
and stepped in the darkness.
He broke off a tooth of the comb
that he was wearing, and lit it.

A ghastly change had come over Izanami.
Covered with innumerable maggots and
surrounded with thunder, she rose and
cried, "How dare you shame me like this!"
Straightaway she dispatched foul-featured
hags from the land of Yomi
to pursue Izanagi.

The army of female demons ran after Izanagi.
These she-devils were so fleet of foot they
could leap a thousand miles at a stride.

Running as fast as he could,
Izanagi took his headdress and
cast it down. Once it hit the
ground, the headdress was
instantly transformed
into delicious grapes.

whereupon they
instantly turned
into bamboo sprouts.

Still they pursued him.
Izanagi took the toothed comb
from his hair, broke it and
cast down the pieces

Izanagi finally reached the base of the Even Pass of Yomi. He plucked the magical peaches that were growing there and threw them at his pursuers. They all turned and fled back to Yomi.

Therefore Izanagi designated the peach tree the Great-Divine-Fruit.

Seeing her army retreat,
Izanami, the mighty one,
pursued Izanagi herself.

So Izanagi drew the
Thousand-Draught
Rock and
blocked up
the Even Pass
of Yomi.

From the other
side Izanami
spoke,

"My beloved
one, if you
do this,
I will
strangle
one
thousand
people
of your
land
every
day."

Izanagi replied, "My lovely wife, if you do this, I will build one thousand five hundred birthing houses everyday."

Now they are separated eternally. This is why the daily average of births exceeds that of deaths.

Izanagi came back to Japan, which was covered in light. Izanagi bathed in a river to purify his mighty body. Many deities were born from his clothes and belongings.

When Izanagi washed his left eye, Amaterasu Oomino Kami, the Sun Goddess, was born. When Izanagi washed his right eye, Tsukuyomi no Mikoto, the Moon God, was born. When Izanagi washed his nose, Susanoo no Mikoto, Male Augustness, was born.

Izanagi trembled with joy. "I finally have these illustrious children."

These three gods who were born from Izanagi's purification became Japan's guardian deities and are still worshiped with great respect today.

Author's Note

The Kojiki, completed in 712 C.E., is Japan's oldest surviving written work. It was produced in three volumes that cover the mythology and establishment of the nation of Japan. These volumes are divided loosely corresponding to myth, legend, and actual historical events. The Kojiki is not only an invaluable historical source and entertaining compilation of Japanese mythology, it is also the cornerstone of the Japanese indigenous Shinto religion, its gods and rituals. The stories are spectacular, exotic, mysterious and sometimes even comical. I focused on producing an artist's book about the beginning of the story, the creation myth.

Shimane Prefecture in Japan has the strongest ties to the mythology of the Kojiki and it is also where my house is located. A third of all the places mentioned in the myths are located in my prefecture and I have visited many of them. Thus, I have had my own experiences reflecting on the Kojiki, and many of them I have incorporated into this book. Since the Kojiki is so closely related to Shimane Prefecture, there are more religious rituals and events throughout the year there than in most other regions. Each community has its own tradition of performing Kagura, which literally means "God entertainment" at their festivals. Kagura refers to a specific type of sacred Shinto theatrical dance set to music that is dedicated to the deities in the mythology. My sons grew up dedicating their dancing to the gods during the festivals at our village shrine.

There is a unique pluralistic attitude to religion in Japan, which has deeply informed our traditions and culture. We see Shinto shrines and Buddhist temples all over Japan and it is not uncommon for them to coexist in the same space. Shinto is an extremely tolerant religion and over many centuries, Buddhism and Christianity were accepted in Japan with little conflict, though with some political dissent. Buddhism spread rapidly in the 6th century and the Japanese adopted it along with Shintoism. This approach inspired my decision to use the image of my favorite Buddhist statue, Gigei-ten of Akishino Temple in Nara, as the face of the Shinto god Izanagi in the purification scene. There are more than eight million gods and goddesses in Japan that inhabit the world as a variety of spirits and other manifestations. This includes human-shaped deities like Izanagi and Izanami in this book, as well as animals. There are also many other types of deities representing nature and weather such as oceans, mountains, winds, rain and thunder. They all coexist and surround us in Japan.

This artist's book was completed at the University of Iowa Center for the Book in April 2018.

The text and images were initially printed on handmade paper made by the artist using flax, cotton and Japanese kozo fibers. Areas of selected images were dyed with indigo, black beans, logwood, hibiscus and iron. The images were letterpress printed using linoleum, polymer, and other relief methods. Selected images were stenciled using pochoir applied by hand. The text of Izanagi and Izanami's marriage scene at the pillar is from the book *The Kojiki: An Account of Ancient Matter*, translated by Gustav Heldt, published in 2014, used with permission.

The artist is deeply grateful to her thesis committee, her instructors, and her classmates at the UI Center for the Book. Thanks to Russell Maret, and to the master craftsmen in Japan for their help. Special thanks to Gustav Heldt.

This project was generously supported by a grant from the Caxton Club of Chicago.

—Kazumi Wilds

ABOUT TUTTLE:
"Books to Span the East and West"

Our core mission at Tuttle Publishing is to create books which bring people together one page at a time. Tuttle was founded in 1832 in the small New England town of Rutland, Vermont (USA). Our fundamental values remain as strong today as they were then—to publish best-in-class books informing the English-speaking world about the countries and peoples of Asia. The world has become a smaller place today and Asia's economic, cultural and political influence has expanded, yet the need for meaningful dialogue and information about this diverse region has never been greater. Since 1948, Tuttle has been a leader in publishing books on the cultures, arts, cuisines, languages and literatures of Asia. Our authors and photographers have won numerous awards and Tuttle has published thousands of books on subjects ranging from martial arts to paper crafts. We welcome you to explore the wealth of information available on Asia at www.tuttlepublishing.com.

Published by Tuttle Publishing, an imprint of Periplus Editions (HK) Ltd.

www.tuttlepublishing.com

Copyright © 2019 Periplus Edition (HK) Ltd.
Illustrations © 2019 Kazumi Wilds
Library of Congress Cataloging-in-Publication Data is in process.

ISBN 978-4-8053-1539-2

23 22 21 20 19   06 05 04 03 02 01

Printed in Hong Kong   1906EP

Distributed by:
North America, Latin America and Europe
Tuttle Publishing,
364 Innovation Drive,
North Clarendon,
VT 05759-9436.
Tel: 1 (802) 773 8930
Fax: 1 (802) 773 6993
info@tuttlepublishing.com
www.tuttlepublishing.com

Japan
Tuttle Publishing
Yaekari Building, 3rd Floor
5-4-12 Osaki, Shinagawa-ku,
Tokyo 141-0032
Tel: (81) 3 5437 0171
Fax: (81) 3 5437 0755
sales@ tuttle.co.jp
www.tuttle.co.jp

Asia Pacific
Berkeley Books Pte Ltd
3 Kallang Sector #04-01,
#02-12 Singapore 349278.
Tel: (65) 6741 2178
Fax: (65) 6741 2179
inquiries@periplus.com.sg
www.periplus.com

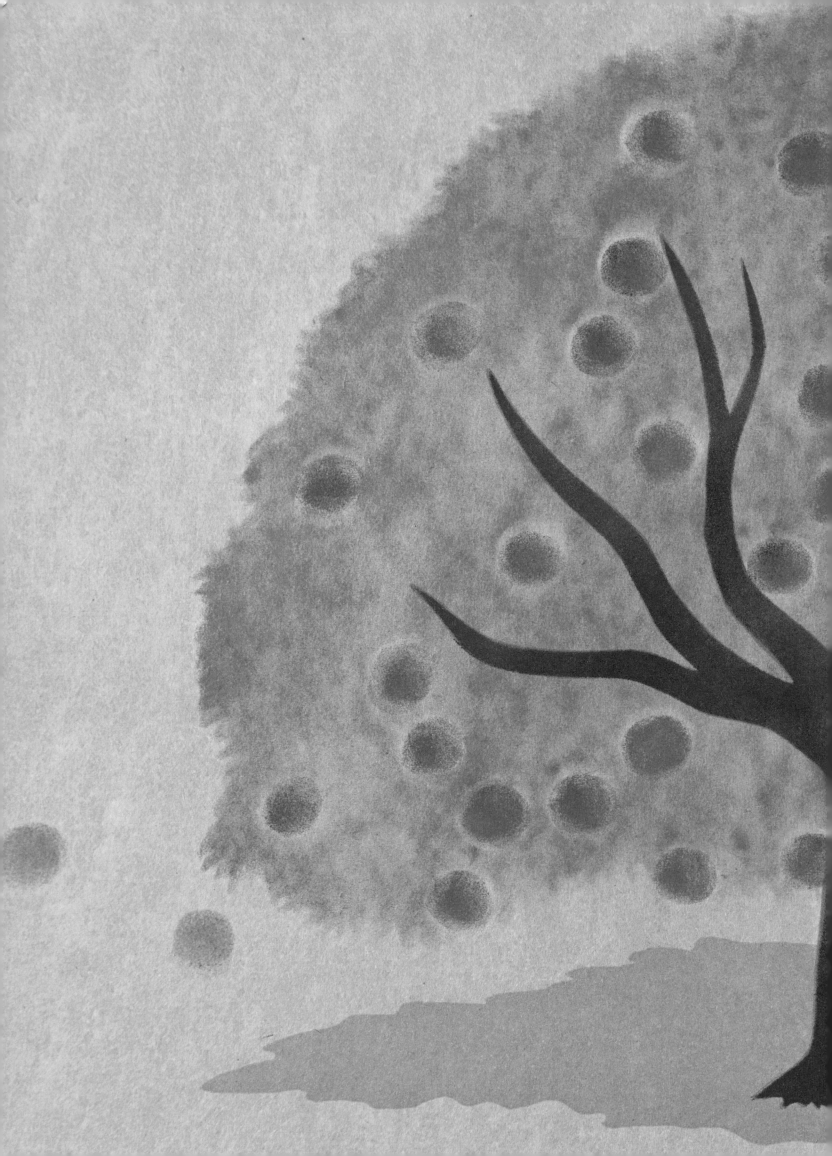